POINTS OF ENTRY

POINTS OF ENTRY

Amy Plettner

WSC | PRESS

ACKNOWLEDGEMENTS

"Saying Good-Bye to His Melancholy," *Misbehaving Nebraskans*, 2017.

"Port" and "Realistic Dream," *Bared*, Les Femmes Folles Books, 2016.

"Provincetown Cemetery," *The Sow's Ear Poetry Review*, 2015.

"Kiss Me," "What It Takes To Conceive," and "Kiss Me, Here," *burntdistrict*, 2014.

"Branched Oak, First Zazen," *Prairie Wind*, Nebraska Zen Center, spring 2014.

"Church Bulletin," *Rattle*, June 2014.

"To My Husband (ex)," *Toe Good Poetry*, 2011.

Forgive ourselves and others
for everything
we needed to do in order to learn.

—Kassi Riordan

TABLE OF CONTENTS

STAGE ONE

STAGE TWO

STAGE THREE

STAGE FOUR

POINTS OF ENTRY

STAGE ONE
gentle against my sleep

The West Room of My Body

It's winter, and I want to turn off my furnace.
Last night I accidentally fell asleep
under wool blankets wearing a long-sleeved shirt.
Woke at two AM to a sweat,
and a third grade classmate, Lorraine Berzi.
No moon slivered the southern horizon.
I thought of my mother, Alice, and Aunt Ann as girls
sleeping together in the upstairs of the farmhouse,
the place we called the west room.
I could see the light of their candle—
my mother the younger of the two.
I can't make out what's covering their feet.
The stairs are steep, a mountain pass;
Donner, or Widow, or Devil's Tail.

My mother just turned six. My Aunt Ann is thirteen.
It's December 27th 1939. My bed is too warm
for my forty-four years. No wind, an unusual night.
My Grammy's at the bottom of the stairs,
her green eyes glint in the wick's light.
She gives her voice to the mountain,
I love you, goodnight.

Her daughters scramble into one bed;
a quick jump, hot water jugs at their feet,
a huddle, a pulling around oneself, each other,
and then, they are perfect. They do not move.
The heat comes close. I sweat and think of my mother
who is seventy-four, my aunt who is eighty-one.
I think of their girlish voices, their sister differences,

their fears that dared them in the dark, their laughter.
They sleep with the rage of Nebraska winds
in a wooden house where coyote song comes in
like stereo sound through the windows rattling glass.

They're my matriarchal fire, my restless sleep,
my bags under the green eyes, my repeated prayer,
my curved left toe, my chin whiskers, my immunity.
I wake on my side with my mother's six-year-old back
curled and pressed into my chest, my stomach, my heart.
My aunt is tight against my spine, her thirteen-year old breasts
are slight, but noticeable against my shoulders.
The night has been full of faces.

The furnace doesn't click on, cranked down to fifty.
I sweat between the child of my mother
and the adolescence of my aunt. I'm my Grammy's age.
I'm searching for the waned moon,
that last thread of light that warms my eyelids
like the tips of their many fingers gentle against my sleep.

1990

—after Ruth Stone

I wore a cotton skirt
thin as my father's handkerchiefs.
How sober I was: such eyes.

Berlin, the Dom Hotel,
a south bay window
where we rocked our sunlit skin.

You had the thick black hair of a native
though you were white as suds,
and German as the brats.

We were near the square;
small pubs, sculptures, street repairs.
We walked amid the broken walls
once separating east from west.
Gypsies, graffiti,
goats grazing in empty lots.

We moved like a pair
of Canada geese on tranquil water
as if our goslings were between us.
We were drifting on a subway of lust.

You were so rugged smoking Marlboros
and stealing bibles from hotel drawers
written in your indigenous tongue.
The air smelled of sausage and sex.

Our dumbfounded history of heritage
exploded from our mouths when we kissed
and the swollen world
pierced us with its fatal charm.

What It Takes to Conceive

Biting kisses, rolling in wet fields,
hours of talking beneath moonlight,
a little wine, dirt, radishes,
brown eggs gathered from the morning lay,

rainy afternoons of Moody Blues,
fresh cut hay, geraniums' flashy blooms,
apple kuchen, coffee, and wood smoke.

The way steep narrow stairs hum
with weight of our feet, and outside
trees umbrella the paved road.

Voices come to us in night,
and we grasp their meaning.
There's an altar in the garden,
Mary Mother of God, but I'm not
Catholic, and can be so wrong.

Forgetfulness—the insignificant fact
of not being married when our daughter
was born. How others treated us with disdain,
and sent up prayers for the sin of us.

It took your thick black hair,
stocky thighs, the harmonica,
and the swinging of Grossmama's good arm
as we sang around her bed in German
I knew without study,

and my mustache as wetness of sea
clung to soft hairs under my nose,
and how you'd lean into me to taste salt,
our bodies sculpting the warm sand.

Sometimes I forget what it took for us
to make our daughter, who grew
your long torso, and strong head.
Whose square face holds
beauty of the Rhine,
and the tearing down of Berlin's wall.
She's a love that forgives ours,
that brings things back to the light.

Winter Ghost

Sunday afternoon, and I'm ready for nine inches
as my daughter and I cluster near wood burner
talking movies and men.

A woman's voice near the kitchen faucet interrupts,
says, *agua*, as the lid to my Grandma's pan
comes out of the dish rack.

Did you hear that? That voice?

I nod my head. Our dogs don't bark.

I told you Mom, I told you,
I'm not crazy. You heard it too.

    I never said I didn't.

I go to the sink, look down at the drain
as if answers will surface
from the aquifer of my ancestors,
gurgle up from an after-life
somewhere below this wooden floor,
this hole cut in the earth.

    I'm here,

but how can I help when I'm stuck in this body,
this life? My prayers take shapes;
a whittled shoe, a lock of mane,
the faded ribbon of my Grammy's corsage.

I place the lid back, draw a glass of water,
leave it for the woman who thirsts.

MOTHER WIT

Pacific pulls sand
from under my feet
and your eyes
focus to sound
of gulls and fog horn.
Eyes color of bull kelp,
moss, sensimilla.

Mist engulfs us
like thick dough.
I stand still for hours
at the headlands
while sea palms cling to stone
and bend in supple postures—

thirty years I've grown
in this skin, a mother now,
who tries to hold you,
you're three, a tad taller
than the seagull
who follows if you turn
your back.

I let you get too far away.
The shore is rough rock,
the tide teases.
Someone please
watch me, stay close,
I've never been
responsible. Lets run,
moon full, beach empty,
cormorants, and our lone fire.

My mind a tangled
forest of kelp broken free.
We kick up sand,
throw off our shirts.
I don't need your father's
hand. Cliffs rise,
waves pull out,
return. You get ahead of me
and moonlight turns you
color of abalone
as if a dream,
and like ocean waves
you pound
tearing away,
and circling back.

NUDE

My daughter says before the family arrives,
you better take down the orgasmic woman, Mom

(a framed drawing near my claw-foot tub).
She's drowning, I say, and walk out,

leaving the sacred presence of our woman-ness
alone in falling sun. My daughter is proven right,

but instead of the orgasmic, drowning woman
it's a copy of Edgar Degas' *The Bath* above my bed:

a woman's backside as she steps into the tub.
Already my basket of erotic literature

has been packed away, out of sight,
but no, it's my most beautiful piece of art

I'm asked to take down or cover up
because the husband wouldn't like it

if their four year old son noticed.
I could've said, *no*. I could've told the child

the painting was of a shorebird
in a green lush forest, stepping into a pond.

A bird that looks a lot like your mother,
and when she hunts, the stillness of her body

slows her heart, and she becomes something larger,
and freer than your Daddy's rules, and when she lifts

into the golden dusk, god is there
to welcome her, to show her another way.

Daughter Floats Above Me

She stands near my bed, startles my dreamy sleep.
The full moon gives shape to her figure
as she says, *I died, watched myself eat.*
Didn't think I'd make it back.

I knock books to the floor,
make a place for her next to me.
I have no cure, no motherly words,
nothing but my hand.

Her blood sugar's so low it doesn't register.
I keep my mouth shut, knowing
she won't remember or care by morning.
I'm glad she made it through

for she's describing the place my mind has gone
since she was ten: of ketoacidosis, diabetic coma,
the place where she will no longer return.

She's a few days away from leaving
for the first time in eighteen years,
and I praise the moon for this daughter,
who woke and ate and came once more to my side.

Harvest

Before pears drop,
and dragonflies
gather for migration.

Before goldenrod turns on
its yellow siren
feeding beetles:
soldier, locust, and blister.

Before cicadas soften
their prolific pulsations,
and purple thistle opens.

Before milkweed pods
split, and sphinx moths
hover for nectar.
Before barn swallows depart,
and tomatoes ripen—

an oncologist opens her,
a furrow in a vast
grassland.

STAGE TWO
like a bastard moon

Realizing My Longest Physical Relationship Is with a Woman (Kassi, My Massage Therapist)

Your touch is written in my skin.
All these years massaging my feet
letting my energy fly into your solar plexus.

You're the only one who believes me
as I go on about my left ovary acting up.
You take me seriously, give me a name
for this sensation, when others laugh.

You say my husband has attached himself
to my left hip. You plant in me *the truth*
which sounds at first like far off drift of dove,
and then is recognizable as my own,
my own voice, the way my mother or father
would recognize it over miles of phone line.
The dormant life of all that I press away
to please others, you awaken,
awaken a desire in me stronger than fear.
Teach me to practice a lost language.

You make a kind of love to me, never once
minimizing my feet, how they scream
and beg for attention or my life forces, shut down,
by trying to be a wife like my mother.
No, you coach me as I release men
from my body in an act of forgiveness.

You show me how to create a protective shield,
expand my energy across the street, into the sky.
I become red-tail, rabbit, mule, grateful
for animal-wisdom. You give me comfort

of words to speak in presence of ghosts,
a spiritual mind to cut strings where needed,
and be rid of tethers to money.

All that society regurgitates into my mouth
you help me sort out, guide me, and as moon sets,
I feel your fingertips press into mine.

Saying Good-Bye to His Melancholy

I talk to myself:
don't take him personally.

I don't listen, get angry,
and flip him the bird.

He doesn't like
identifying anything
with wings,

and my days are full
of kestrel, quail, killdeer,
on this crease of marriage
where miracles of flight
are pressed down,

and the vows
that moved across my lips
didn't say anything
about being your mother.

I won't remind you
to brush your teeth before bed
or change your underwear.

You tell me,
take it easy in bed.

I say, *leave,
unhook your suffering
from my winged hips.*

Points of Entry

Your skin doesn't separate you from the world, it's a bridge through which the external world flows into you and you flow into it.
—Alan Watts

A co-worker introduces me to a man holding a glass of wine,
voices around us loud as a chicken coop with an intruder.

He asks what I do on the prairie. *I hike, walk, let my feet
do acupuncture to the earth*. He thinks I'm doing scientific research,

wants to know how I measure the points of entry,
the sites at which my feet communicate with soil.

He believes me. It's the first time someone really believes me,
other than my friend, Kassi, and now I'm on uneven ground.

Most of my life has been this way, but I'm used to it now,
crave it in fact. I find the paved path sterile and lifeless.

I long for the gully wash out, the narrow cut groove
cattle carve in summer to the tank. I step, imagine a cloven hoof.

If trail thins I lift one foot in front of other like the way my family mimics
Miss America contestants or models on the runway. There's a definite response

from earth, my feet keep it moving under me, it calls my name.
I lay myself against her, bare my chest, let my heart beat press to the grasses,

to the living darkness below. There's a strange communion
with my skin, the thirst of ancestors who broke the prairie on which I now breathe;

they thought they were taking care of the land, their families, me, but they were
killing, killing it, though the land took no revenge, kept on giving, and giving

through generations— streams, pastures, power of wind, wild game,
fruit trees, crops, and stripped cobs for the fire.

This earth is my body, is your body, and if the bible is right
we're made of it, a pinch of dust, clay, sand, organisms,

and I've tasted it, this death and life at our feet, so I'll love
the path, the intellect of my toes, how they connect

like depth of compass plant roots, a strong hold in an eternal cord.
There's no stopping the intention of my feet. I'm sturdy, strong,

fed really, by the very gravity of my connection here,
and my words may be simple, but there's a sophistication in walking

on earth, knowing we need one another. I tell the man,
I walk, that's what I do.

National Poetry Festival,
Des Moines, Iowa 2003

Ruth Stone takes the dim-lit stairs,
feels her way along the bend of wall.

She does it for poetry's sake,
not for pity's sake or mis-take.

She does it because she knows
how obstinate the words can be.

How she'll come to see the square poem
form in her mind. How her fingers

will still be reaching for the edges
where rhythm takes over,

comes to her over the clothes line,
opens her into a daughter's painting,

brush strokes the frightened places
that wait like cardinals before dawn to sing.

And when poets can't see
they lay back ever so gently—

begin to smell the skin of those
around them, breathe in, breathe out,

and what used to have form, and shape,
and pattern leans down, face on top of page

breathing air into the written word,
with a scent of new vision.

New as the words one will find
when unable to depend

on sight alone to do the work.
Poetry, don't let me down—

be that old stubborn rhythm of bone
taking one more step, out, into the dark.

A Single Mother Experiences Western Medicine

In her hand a beige stone.
She's naked, except
for a white sheet
draping her bent legs.

A man comes
to find her vein.
He covers her
breasts with the sheet.

She says, *I don't want pitocin.*
Is there pitocin in there?

She pulls the sheet off her chest,
I don't want it. Makes me sick.

He's thinking, *come on,*
this is a hospital. In the next room
a married couple is about to have
their first son.

He takes the stone from her hand,
feels his own blood beat at his temples.

Pitocin makes me sick.
I don't want it.

But his crystal bag of fluids
hangs above her
like a bastard moon.

Set Jell-O and Cool Milk

My mother stands in the dining room,
puts voice to memory. She's back on the farm

heading to the pump-house, a Mason quart jar
in each hand; one of Jell-O, one of fresh milk.

It's mid-morning, sun batters down,
wind a mere pulse from the south.

She cradles one jar under her arm,
pulls open the misfit wooden door.

A cool dark hesitation in her step,
strains her eyes, and listens for a rattler.

The fear moves out as her skin gives in
to damp air. She pushes up her sleeve,

checks the zinc lids for tightness,
stretches on toes, and bows to immerse

jars, fingers, elbow into the barrel of cold
water drawn from the ground.

She runs a brisk hand over her forehead
to smooth strays loose from her summer braid.

She's of the windmill, of harness,
of chickens, of gathering cobs.

Now her mother's beside her
in the kitchen, a warm heel of buttered

graham bread placed into her mouth.
She chews, and swallows, sustenance, life;

the salubrious value of work, of farm,
of set Jell-O and unspoiled milk come supper.

NEARING FIFTY

May we all become, someday, perfectly useless and beautiful.
    —John G. Neihardt

Someday I'm going to be somebody,
like today, in my kitchen
as my Mom teaches my daughter
to master the pressure canner.
Thirteen quarts of beets later
I can look into their steady faces,
and want nothing.

And it's the thirteen-lined ground squirrel
hunkered down in my backyard,
in scorching heat,
switching its tail, ready to pounce,
that makes the day's purpose.

And someday I'm going to be somebody.
While others travel the world
seeing the natural wonders, I'll sketch
the tussock moth caterpillar,
walk dewless grasses of July,
track ant lion's craters.

While others make their marks
conquering the mountain,
I'll be counting eastern tailed-blues
and watching dragonflies launch
their eggs into still-green pond.

While others seek stamps
on their passports, I'll sink my feet
deep into my hiking boots,
and stay home.

Kiss Me, Here

I want you to kiss me, but not
in front of your mother
or at the altar
or beside your old lover.

I want you to kiss me
with your tongue,
but not with
the other woman's
children peering
from their mattress
on the floor.

I want you to kiss me
on my ear, from behind
while my hands are in
hot suds at the kitchen sink,
cinch your arms around
my hips, pin me,
but not while my fingers
feel for the sharp knives.

I want you to kiss-kiss me
on the hollow of my arch,
feel your beard between
my toes, want my lips to taste
of blood, wrists to bruise blue.
I want you to blow me
those breathy kisses that come.

Pre-Menopausal

This is not a place to get drunk and smoke and fuck around—
no, this is a place where I get naked in winter near wood burner

as south sun penetrates glass, heats skin while I lay on the couch purchased just for
the cave, just for me, the kama sutra couch I call it. My body against scarlet fabric

shocking as a cardinal against the snowy field. I listen to music, quiet stuff
my daughter loaded on my iPod and I read poems by Sharon Olds and Robert Bly

and William Stafford. I write a poem. I'm the author of this world, no longer waiting
for my husband to become available for intimacy, no, I have it within myself— intimacy

with lady beetles, shrikes, the weight of wood I carry to make warmth. I move
and that creates an intimacy with my breath, my mind. I relearn how to walk

and there's as much pleasure in my steps as when I was ten months old. Sometimes I fall.
Sometimes I walk backwards and miss the narrow path, find myself eye to eye with big

bluestem. I'm of the seasons confident my estrogen and my eggs and my elasticity of skin are
drying like native grasses in a Nebraska winter and there seems nothing more

appropriate than the rough hands of my years touching the smooth vibrant skin of my daughter,
pregnant, and I tickle her arm the way I did when she was small. The cracked

flesh of my fingertips give a gentle scratch. We exchange this touch and I'm not sorry for my
weathered skin because here I am, alive, in my cave, my mystery, not my mother

or sister or friends but the place where I heal and rage and weep and make love and create with or
without eggs. I've spent all this time accommodating my body, supporting

and making decisions about the potential life I carry and there's no end to my fertility when I
gather at the table and see the beauty of the women my daughters have become.

CHURCH BULLETIN

The singing has already started,
and I stand in the back. My family's heads
lined up in two pews near the front,
same pews for forty years.
It looks as though a small child
sits between my sister and her husband

but it's really just a canyon
stretching its massive void, and what a great thing
to be able to say; *you're working on the marriage,*
instead of just in it, stuck, like logs
jammed in the river.

My brother's wife is missing altogether.
She's socializing with the millionaires
who can give her more than God.
Sometimes the church is like a bar—

all that light as powerful in its clarity
as the darkness, and my siblings' hair
is now many shades of cloudy sky.
They've transformed into adults, parents,
survivors, divorcees, forgetting at times
how to play, and open, and feel.

The church says, for joys,
Lord in your love, and for tragedy, *Lord
in your mercy.* Dad is closest to the aisle,
a quick escape, and Mom is shorter,
smaller, so much smaller. I walk to the family pew
taking my place among what's easily broken.

Close enough now to see my parents hands
each with matching bruises on the thin skin
beneath the knuckles. How has this day come?

The pastor is into his sermon
beginning with a clip of *The Lion King*,
and I think of my daughter at four years old
standing on the arm of the couch
in our apartment on 16th and Washington
holding up her stuffed lion, Simba, to the sun,
the way Rafiki does in the movie, and I'm a single
unwed mother on welfare, the woman
my Dad likes to rage of, and I've been to the well,
and the river, and the pump, and know my baptism
has come, and I am fully a part of this.

In-between the Chemo

Kassi's massaging my hands
when she says, *Aunt Carol's death*
leaves you all alone in your family.
I hold up my arm,
and every hair's standing.

I ask if she's lost hers. We look.
Touch her skin—
smooth as a round milky stone,
not a hair, or an eyelash or a stray
anywhere, stripped clean,
every follicle hollow.

The last thing she does
is run her oiled palms and fingers
across my forehead,
down each side of my jaw,
and out over my ears.
I hear an ocean pull away.

STAGE THREE

flooding with blue roots

LIFE'S COCKTAIL

You steal the bible for me,
wrap it in brown paper towels,
deep in your non-belief.

We see nothing but each other,
attracted by the configuration of our hands
each lifeline intersecting at precise curve
where our pasts collide and spin away.

I wake to a soft-boiled egg
held up in a stemmed glass cup
as if a single flower in a vase,
a brown shell against floral wallpaper
and a handwritten note.

Your uncle wears slippers thin
from the war. I wear a rayon dress
to city shore, purple,
embroidery at the hem, no panties.
Because of the bible I refuse to marry.

Our first time on a nude beach,
staring at gay couples,
and the woman with large floppy cap
whose toddler suckles in its shade.
We cover ourselves with sand,
race to rinse off in rolling water.

I drink shots of eggnog liqueur
sprinkled with coffee grounds,
make it up steep attic stairs

without a sprain. Berlin's contempt
soothed by the artist's blood.

East Germany steals back its flair for color.
Cars line up for miles, drivers smoke,
and play cards on hoods of vehicles
as they wait for fuel. I recover a bicycle

abandoned in haymow, ride dusty roads
on a seat of metal. I make a nest of moonlight
when nights bring no rest.
When the train pulls away I know
I'll never see Aunt Betel again.
Getting everything I wanted
was the worst thing that happened .

PROVINCETOWN CEMETERY

I'm trying to follow the smell of whiskey,
breath of the dead, but the sandy path
leads me to Mary beloved wife
and Captain William Chester Sparrow.

I'm hunting for Stanley Kunitz and Norman
following directions from Tim's Used Books:
Go right at the T, they're in the same area,
take whiskey for Mailer, it's catching on.

My daughter asks why I care about a man
I never read and one I never knew?
What good is it to stand before a name,
holding an empty bottle?

But it's Stanley's fingers I fell for
when I was on my knees in the stacks
and opened *The Wild Braid.*
Perhaps it makes no sense,

but in the pictures earth clung
under his nails, staining his fingertips,
the veins in his hands
flooding with blue roots.

As My Marriage Falls Apart

My longing lies in mauve bloom
of milkweed, in cut alfalfa
fragrant with heavy sunshine,
in bluebirds quick shimmer
over ground plum and chokecherry.

The skirting of butterfly wings
along the uncut edge of fence
lined in raging pink
and scraggly mulberry.

A line I once crossed
before knowing the sky
was a trillion shades of ocean
and one lone turkey buzzard
can blot out the sun just long enough
to make me think of second chances.

Across a stretch of brome
a killdeer feigns a broken-wing
as our red heeler, Buddy, falls for the act.
Four eggs, color of wet sand,
specked black, lie protected
in the nest of white rock,
woodchips, and crabgrass.

The killdeer lifts,
returns undetected
to sit under a quiet moon,
her mate echoing over the fields,
stay, stay, stay.

Realizing that what my mother told me was the truth. That no one, anywhere, can shake my joy.

PROOF

Below the sawhorse in the barn
next to a tin Folgers coffee can
is a brown paper sack
wrapped around a fifth of brandy—
three-fourths gone.

A wife who found the fifth
is one hundred proof beyond reaction.
The bottle not yet sure
whose life it has emptied.

ACCIDENTAL DISCOVERY OF THE AUTOMATIC KEN BURNS EFFECT

The Ken Burns effect feature enables a widely used technique of embedding still photographs in motion pictures, displayed with slow zooming and panning effect, and fading transitions between frames.
    —Wikipedia

Tom Waits' voice accompanies our faces,
movements near water—

our bodies ebb and flow
with language of ocean.

All day Buddha listens to the snail.

We embrace each other like barnacles,
until we're torn away.

Bare feet on paths near poppies—

we praise the plums by packing our cheeks,
stuff them full.

Eucalyptus and fog,
the fence broken in rattlesnake grass,

a man's hand
suspended above his cup
for eternity.

Under the Elms

I see her black-bottomed cowgirl boots
dangling over a low branch,
smooth line of her jawbone
framed in soft twigs and supple
green-toothed leaves. Overhead,
sunlight plays. Her hair,
dark walnut strung with honey
combs through the breeze like a tangled
shadow. She's up there drawing,
drawing the last days of summer.
A cloudless blue rush of south wind
pushes her pencil; traces waterfall,
bison, gulch, log, sage. I'm her mother, guilty
of not enough days like this one
where the cotton sheet is spread
beneath elms along an old corner of fence.
I give her to the sway of wind and tree
that holds her now, that rocks her above me,
understanding how it is come fall
when the simple leaves
must let go of their branches.

EPHEMERAL

Moonlight is a type of language
And the hills at night call my name, my name
And every grasshopper along the path
Is certain of what death will come
Within this forest of November grass
And the sharp *peel* of the great horned owls'
Voice straightens me into reverie.
I feel my prayers believed.

Ovariectomy

I see Kassi in the oncologist office,
hearing; *we'll leave the port in*
just for safe measure,
but looks like you're good.

She asks the oncologist,
do you want some eggs
(the oncologist appears confused).

She asks again, *do you want some eggs*
and reaches into her cloth bag,
pulls out a carton— ivories,
greenish-blues, every shade of brown.

She tells the story of *doctor down,*
doctor down, as oncologists aren't used
to trades of fresh-made croissants or eggs
warm from the hen at sunrise.

Mamma Came Back as a Snake

A photo by Dorothea Lange, 1937

My sister and I kept it a secret from Daddy.

We hiked out to the west range in a blast of mirages and sage,
stumbled upon large stones, uncovered her.

She only visited in dead of afternoon
taking protection from heat under our tar paper shanty.

Daddy always left us with a barrel of water,
and he'd crank up the car, take off in his polished shoes.

Never understood why his old boots
sat along the bench outside our only door.

He said it was field-work, but his pants
were clean, shirt pressed. Nothing looked right

in Daddy's hands after mamma died.
I'd watch him pick up Charlotte,

and it was as if she were a chunk of wood, or worse,
that dead coyote he threw off the main road.

A disjointed hand, no longer attached to the man
my mamma loved to tease with a tussle of his thick black hair.

He used to smile and laugh, laugh the way you hear coyotes
in their joy, their bliss of hunt as if all his senses were keen,

intact, ripe, ready to burst out in his rapture to this woman,
my mamma. I stand in the doorway peek around the flap of cardboard.

I saw myself in the mirror on Daddy's car once,
and wondered about my face. It reminded me of the stone by the creek,

the one we rolled away to uncover mamma and bring her home.

For My Husband (ex)

I want to bring him down
to the woods where morels burst in spring,
earth smells of hemlock, and nettle.
I want to bring him out
of his bedroom's darkening shades,
face him toward morning meadow.

I want to bring him to life
in the dust, beneath a stone—
a click beetle, a gold-eyed toad.
I want to bring him pumice,
wash his hands of nicotine and fuel,
rub his knuckles with almond oil,
bring his clean palm to my cheek.

I want to bring him a new flannel shirt,
bed sheets smelling of lavender wind.
I want to take him to the stream
where I'll go belly down in mud,
invite the boy in him to follow,
make cups out of our bodies,
hands full of water, and sun.

My Father and Daughter Dance

I'm standing outside the First Presbyterian Church.
All around me are people I love or have hated
and loved again. Everyone's waiting for my daughter.

She'll be the one in white, the bride, the wife.
I'm hungry, my gut empty, and I'm reminded
of the morning I left the hospital twenty-three years ago.

My caseworker carried my daughter out the front.
I took the fire escape. There were no bouquets to carry.
The stairwell was a cold gray echo of footsteps,

and when I pushed open the door that forced me into April,
an abrupt jolt from dim to fabulous light, I wanted to run.
I could hear the traffic on Highway 30.

My mom and sister put me in the car. I stared out
the window of clear glass and saw nothing.
They drove me home. I couldn't recognize the feel of my pillow.

This was no longer my head. Someone else parted my hair.
Today the hollow in my belly becomes a canyon
graced in light. I see my father with his stooped back

stand in a line holding a dollar. He waits
until the D.J. says, *switch*, and he steps forward
to take his first-born grandchild's hand.

A Cold Day, and an Old Man

In morning fog he comes to me.
His shoulders hunched, caving in on themselves,
right foot crossing into path of his left
to catch the pitch of his body.
We speak after seasons of endless rain.
His fingers sag near an overweight heart,
and I remember the hollow echo of oars.

My voice is thunder, hard wind. In this moment
my words hang, a torn branch from his ear.
I say too, *I love you*, and these three fall
like dry wings of beetles to fill cracks in the wood floor.
He wears a lavender shirt. Winter has bitten his hands.
He asks me to button his collar.
My fingers are that of a woman. This startles me.

PORT

When Kassi raises
her arms at her office,

The Center For Well-Being,
smiling; *I'm cancer free,*

and I see the bulge
near her heart chakra
just under the skin—

she touches it then
with her hand
catching my stare,

doctor wants to leave it,
just in case.

Two months later,
the growth
is back.

Oncologist saying,
there's nothing
more to be done.

Treatment's
your life.

STAGE FOUR
it was passing

Insurance

A glass of water in a spare room,
bare feet on a wood floor.

Every cell has intelligence—
to swallow is to worship.

Breathe, sustain, she says,
it doesn't cost anything.

Psalm 1,991

It's not my Psalm. Not my wilderness.
Not my cave. Not my tears.

—Ken Gere

I've just read
the 140th Psalm,
a Psalm for David,
which turns me
to my Psalm,
when my daughter's
father was tracking
me through city streets
in someone else's car,
wearing sunglasses

and hat to disguise
himself so I wouldn't
call the cops,
and our daughter
was two weeks old,
a May baby, born in the USA
though conceived
in the place of our ancestors
across the ocean
as though we had to put

their immigration in reverse
in order to consummate
our lusty heritage.
Back over the Atlantic,
opposite of the way
our relatives had fled.

We charge back in our youth
and restlessness,
to our German,
hear the old language,

and let its dialect fill us
under the open fields
that stretch from our
Great's villages.
It's the 140th Psalm
I knew one line from
when I was pregnant
and twenty-seven,
and you (my daughter's father)
were suicidal and full of drink.

Afraid I wasn't going
to marry you,
which I didn't,
and so you got
dressed up
like someone else,
forgetting to camouflage
your scent,
the smell of your man-skin
that started all this

in the first place,
and I step up
to the pediatrician's
office door,

and the wind is soft
out of the south,
and amongst the magnolia
blossoms I smell nicotine,
and faint scent
of fried potatoes,

turn to see you
leering behind a tree.
140th Psalm,
though I didn't know it
at the time, is in my mind,
one line, a mantra, a chant—
heap hot coals of kindness,
heap hot coals of kindness
on his head. Is he the enemy?
Is he my love?

This doesn't mean
I'm not honest
or straightforward
or making statements,
it only means I will
treat you the way
I want to be treated,
and my Psalm—
the song of 1991,
Psalm 1,991—

is to be at peace
with myself and my world.

I'm raising a daughter,
now give me peace,
oh, Lord, from the passions
of my past,
from the candlelight
and wine in a castle
in Marburg,
from the stolen bible

he carries in his duffle,
from the way we slip-slam
our skin against the stone
of the church,
from what I saw him take
at the farm, money
he didn't need,
because he could play
his Aunt's compassion
for the siblings

who'd moved away,
the ones torn worse
by the violence of America,
the beautiful.
American husband
who'd stick out
his cane to trip his wife,
your Mom, and she'd bruise,
a bruised apology
in the confines

of that ill house
on 38th Street that sang
both tunes of pure
love and pure lies.
A house where no one's
safe, not even the dog
under the couch.
From this neglect
and fear and evil
was a mind so sharp

and brilliant that I wanted
to somehow wed or weld
with it, commune
in its phenomenal
thinking and creativity.
My daughter's father's mind.
The philosopher, the Far Side
cartoon appreciator,
the music maker, lyrics
all original, the-willing-

to-eat-boiled-land-slugs-
and-call-it-escargot,
though cold tarry liquid
shot between his teeth,
the black ink staining
afternoon's scarlet
geraniums with evil
and we were in love,
because I was
the healer, the one

to mend a torn toe,
to darn the sock, and hold
my hand on your chest
where your father
had left his fists of rage,
and I have not that power,
though I do have love,
and you have not that
power to destroy,
though you do

have evil. So here
we stood,
the two of us,
so wanting to live
under each other's
lips, but instead
me moving out
of fear into self-
preservation,
and you moving out

of fear into control.
I knew only
your destructive
ways were
your worst enemy.
It was never me,
though you liked
to believe
I was plotting
against you.

So I *heap hot coals*
of kindness
on your head,
and they burn
in night, blister
your dreams,
ignite the collar
of your shirt.
Embers singe your

white socks. I love
your evil ways.
I hate your evil ways,
and so I step
back, the way
our ancestors did,
until there's only
ash devils
whirling in late
afternoon sun.

IRREVOCABLE

A Place Whose Time Has Come
—Fallbrook Entrance Sign

Someone sold out.
The horses were hauled away.
People came in bulldozers,
the way surgeons
used to come at a face
to perform a lobotomy
so little left recognizable.
The bodies of cottonwood
ruined, cut off at the ankle.
Roots ripped from earth
like fingers of children
who cling to their parents
as a babysitter tries
to coerce them away.

People heal from the inside
out, but nature doesn't
have a chance in concrete.
The pond is overthrown
and leveled. Pine trees
from another land
are trucked in,
severed and bloodied
to be transplanted
on a constructed ridge
where run-off is inevitable.
The trees can't take the shock
don't make it through the summer.
Enormous three story homes

slap up into the horizon
like an abuse cycle
gone crazy for generations.

When pasture is given
to soil movers,
pond to drainage ditch,
path to sidewalk,
dirt road to asphalt,
old trees to struggling transplants,
horses to 200,000 dollar homes,
pitcher sage and sunflower to petunias,
leaves and blown down branches
to maroon lava rocks,
and native grasses taken over
by true green Chem-lawns;
there's nothing left to say.

The names of the new streets
say it all; Windflower,
Bush Clover, Aster, Nighthawk,
Saltgrass, Blue Sage—
welcome to Fallbrook
just off the Purple Heart Highway.

KASSI BESIDE ME

I walk big and loose for her.
Close my eyes and let my feet
do the looking.

I fool the animals
with my tracks,
go up backwards,
back ass wards.

I stop at a bench
topped with snow
in middle of the prairie,

remove my glove,
sink my finger
into a mound of crystals,

a bare canvas,
and carve out words,
touch has memory.

I take the top ridge.
Nothing's flat here.
The landscape

scarred and gutted.
I scream and turn
downhill on a deer path,

native grasses cut
at my face,
slap at my jacket.

I stay upright
in falling snow.

MOVEMENT OF AIR

—after Wallace Stevens

Among the congregations the only commonality was wind.
I was of three postures like a priest in which there are three forces:

wind that knocks your breath away or blows
coffee from your cup. If it stops, beware.

Here in cottonwood, leaves circle and rush as if rapids of river
and one can see for miles. I do not understand humanity,

is it to pray to be rid of self or to write to be remembered?
The wind in the keyhole or the bulldozer leveling the house.

Stained glass windows filled with pleas and a lone candle.
The push of air beneath our breasts, oh to laugh through our noses,

and extinguish the dark. How many times have we flown
into the clean glass stunned by a landscape of cedar and Quonset sky?

I know men like the red-wing, riding the tip of cattail, making a ruckus,
but I know too that it's done in the name of a woman's solitude.

When the wind spread itself it moved tall grasses
like sticks of beating drums. At the sound of winter's ticking ice

and a pocket of moonlight even the wind sat motionless.
Time is fleeting. The wind must be bound.

It was childhood, all experience, it was passing,
and it was going to pass. The wind wailed in the ponderosas.

Branched Oak, First Zazen

The bell chimes into dark tinsel of stars.
We begin sitting, eyes open, gazing down.

There's incense, snapping of fire. A window
where the moon's full body distracts me—
a wild lover, and I'm trying to keep still.

I can hear the woman next to me swallow.
My friend told me she believed her father's
open-heart surgery, really opened his heart.

Spine is strong as my open gaze,
mind certain as my feet. The grain
in wood floor breaths with me, comes to life.

This room is small as the universe.
We aren't limited to one place.

A hibernating click beetle awakens from a log
just in time to be saved from cremation.
How much time is left before I, too, am fully awake?

Awake to the breath of those around me—
cat, bird, shrew, brother, awake to knuckles
in the hand, soft touching of thumbs,
the oval strength of this moment, now.

Harvey at Five Months

My grandson goes into a trance
once out over threshold of house.

He goes Zen on me.
His crying grunting curses cease

and he begins to open
his vise-grip fists

each knuckle relaxes,
palm opens flat

as he reaches for
a huge heart-shaped

leaf of catalpa,
supple and green.

He's five months old,
wind his only pacifier.

He wants to touch
the bee, the bloom,

and he does it
with slow extension of arm

hand stroking
the humid air.

All morning he studies the paths
of barn swallows

as sun makes its way,
first light catching us at our best—

a full night's sleep
with vivid dreams.

We sit in a wicker chair
hanging from a low branch

as wren scolds
us for our sinful intrusions.

It's Sunday morning
and this is our church,

a stump of locust
cut by his father, our altar.

The aisle is acres of grass.
I keep my bare feet plugged into

the soil and sway
with rhythm of a slight breeze.

We let the hymn
of cardinal and bobwhite

be our prelude and our benediction.
My grandson doesn't fight.

He's still as the dove,
talking at times

to this world
with soft H sounds

like the ohm of a yogi.
He has enlightenment

at his fingertips, his tongue.
His thick thighs not yet ready

to walk or run
but already he knows how to sit

to be with the natural world.
He's born of it—

the breath of grass,
stretch of tree,
the air and sounds

and smell of the permeable earth
forever to cradle him.

While Kassi Exits This World

Pear branches break, a kiss on the back of hand.
Canada geese fly low over house,
wing-grind, pop of my mother's hip.
Tight furrow between eyes, a ball of yarn rolling away.

The bees are tired. Chickens pluck the random earth,
weight of bones pacing room to room,
a leaf floats beyond the front gate and hedges,
rises over cherry trees nippled with tiny buds.

Kiss Me

I want you to.
No, I don't.

I say it, but don't
mean it.

Damn the body, damn
the morning light.

It's all made
for love,

the spider,
and dew-laden web.

See the sun—
it slams against

our bare chests,
weeps

on our pleasure.
Kiss me here,

close your mouth
on my throat.

BRIGHT, THIS BODY

Tonight, I'm afraid
of the dark.

A lunar eclipse,
the smear of blood
onto the test strip,

and I'm stripped
from the uterus, out.

A mother, a mother,
a mother, no longer wife.

Born, unborn,
broken bright.

I'm afraid of the dark.

If I close my eyes
an eclipse of this body

may vanish me.

Receiving the Call, March 6, 2011

The dead don't suffer; it's their time to recover from living.
—Tierno Monenembo

Cluster of starlings wish-over,
a goose abandoned in acres of sky.
Blackbird's twill deepens
to that color of evening blue
my niece loves.
Muskrats work icy edges.

I'm on the quiet bridge.
My hands are tight fists
and I open them
as if opening my eyes to first light
the way Kassi taught me eight years ago
back when I had a television and a husband.
When she sent me home
asking me to pay attention to my hands,
to relax them.

Kassi, you are no longer a body,
and I want to, what? Run, fuck,
cry, sit in the sun.
You take my open hand,
line up your fingertips with mine
press them back, every cell shouting.

REALISTIC DREAM

More than 80,000 chemicals available in the United States have been tested for their toxic effects on our health and environment.

—Natural Resources Defense Council

I want to give my attention to dreams,
in early dawn when the dogs
breathing regulates my sleep.

My daughter in an indigo and orange skirt,
under the pear tree, gathering fruit,
as I busy myself husking sweet corn.
Bees vibrate purple blossoms of thistle.
She calls to me, and collapses.

I go to her. She can't speak.
There's spit at the corner of her mouth.
I scoop her into my arms. I haven't carried her
for fifteen years the way I'm carrying her now
into the house. She can't drink. She needs something:
orange juice or toast with honey,
a cooked potato, anything full of carbs
to raise her blood sugar, fast,
so she can open her eyes, and stare
back at me. I stop the dream,
and sit up to a soft rain, long overdo.

I want to forget: juvenile diabetes,
cystic fibrosis, multiple sclerosis, cancers:
breast, ovarian, pancreas, lung.
I wake in realistic dream to my Aunt Carol's voice
as it grew fainter while Uncle John held her hand
in the rented hospice bed;

to Kassi strolling into the plowed field
as her cherry trees were blooming
to confront the driver of a massive co-op sprayer,
wind eighteen miles an hour, her head bright and bald
as a cue ball from the chemo;

and to the phone conversation, my oldest daughter,
telling me how she took the kids outside
to watch the crop sprayer coming in low to dust
freeways of corn encircling their house,
and the kids, looking up, mouths open in wonder.

I want to forget my Aunt Marie's scars
where her breasts were carried away. Forget,
forget. I want to give my attention to air and sunshine,
to taste of water straight from the pump
where hundreds of acres of native grasses surround the cattle tank
and my feet know not of concrete or harsh poisons,
just the click of grasshopper wing and trill song of dickcissel.

Platte, Early March

I touch the river,
forget my other life.
The cranes talk.

This is not the end!
This is not the end!
they say, all eighty-five thousand,
and their voices

turn my ear to heart
as I lie down in grasses
along the bank
where current moves free

and eagles hold sharp
to cottonwood's naked arms.
A beaver carries a stick
upstream as the thick bed
of clouds breaches blue,

vanishes loneliness.
The kingfisher
sits on last year's branch,
a favorite perch,

and I let loose
beneath the chorus
so ancient and real:
everything,

every single thing,

exists
with or without me.
I've touched
the river, and need
no other life.

ABOUT THE AUTHOR

AMY PLETTNER holds a MFA from the University of Nebraska. She lives and works on a tallgrass prairie in southeast Nebraska where she has learned to wrangle snakes, wasps, and small mammals. Much of her work can be found in an old set of luggage stacked next to her bed that requires no key. Her first book, *Undoing Orion's Belt*, came out in 2011, and her poems have been anthologized in *Nebraska Poetry: A Sesquicentennial Anthology 1867-2017*, *The Untidy Season*, and *Nebraska Presence*.